Fill
The Gap
With Prayer

DRUCILLA WHITE

Fill The Gap With Prayer

© 2021 by Drucilla White

All rights reserved. No portion of this book may be reproduced, stored in a retrieval system, or transmitted in any form or by any means – electronic mechanical, photocopy, recording, scanning, or other – except for brief quotations in critical reviews or articles, without the prior written permission of the publisher.

www.advisedbyamber.com

Printed in the United States of America

ISBN-13: 978-1-7367096-0-3

Scriptures marked KJV are taken from the KING JAMES VERSION (KJV): KING JAMES VERSION, public domain.

Scriptures marked NLT are taken from the HOLY BIBLE, NEW LIVING TRANSLATION (NLT): Scriptures taken from the HOLY BIBLE, NEW LIVING TRANSLATION, Copyright© 1996, 2004, 2007 by Tyndale House Foundation. Used by permission of Tyndale House Publishers, Inc., Carol Stream, Illinois 60188. All rights reserved. Used by permission.

Scriptures marked NIV are taken from the NEW INTERNATIONAL VERSION (NIV): Scripture taken from THE HOLY BIBLE, NEW INTERNATIONAL VERSION ®. Copyright© 1973, 1978, 1984, 2011 by Biblica, Inc.TM. Used by permission of Zondervan Publishing House. All rights reserved.

Scripture quotations are from The ESV® Bible (The Holy Bible, English Standard Version®), copyright © 2001 by Crossway, a publishing ministry of Good News Publishers. Used by permission. All rights reserved.

Eternally In Loving Memory

Bishop Henry Wayne White
My love and husband of 48 years

Deacon Clifford L. Warren and Elder Doretha Warren
My parents

Deacon Son Henry White and Deaconess Mary White
My parents in love

Bishop Clifford Warren, Jr. and Bishop Ronald Warren
My brothers

Rev. Dorothy Huffman, Rev. Mary Lois Hendricks and Bishop Anna Doris Harris
My sisters

Praise for Author Drucilla White

Mother, we are so proud of you and your accomplishment of writing your first book of prayers. We have been blessed to have you as our example and teacher of living out our life through prayer. As far back as we can remember, when we were young, you always made us feel like we too can talk to God and he would hear our prayers. As we have all grown through different challenges, triumphs and disappointments, you taught us to pray and believe that God would see us through. Thank God for a praying Mother!

Proverbs 31:10,28 AMP

"An excellent woman [one who is spiritual, capable, intelligent, and virtuous], who is he who can find her? Her value is more precious than jewels and her worth is far above rubies or pearls." (v. 10)

Her children rise up and call her blessed (happy, prosperous, to be admired); Her husband also, and he praises her... (v. 28)

It is our prayer that every reader that opens this powerful little prayer book is inspired to start or continue a prayer life. It is only through prayer that we experience peace, be free and be whole!

Your loving children,
Hannah, Yvonne and Dwayne

This Prayer Book is dedicated to my Grandchildren

Rachel Diamond Terrell
Jalen Dennis
Craig Matthew Terrell
McKenzie Simone Smith
Dwayne David White
MaKayla Sidney Smith
Aidynn Dru White

Special Thanks and Recognition

Deaconess Betty Jean Carter – Sister

Pastor Donald & Lady Michelle Warren – Brother and Sister (in love)

Sister Lula Odom – Sister (in love)

Hannah Terrell, Yvonne Smith and Dwayne White – Children

Amber Morson – Editor and Publisher

Son (in love) Craig Terrell and daughter (in love) Lashaunda White

Higher Praise Worship Center Pastor and members

Church of the Living God (Jewell Dominion)

Victory Christian Fellowship Choir

Nieces and nephews

Spiritual Sons and daughters

Ode to A Prayerful Grandmother

Oh, to feel your compassionate touch
At all times, I feel a presence that which comforts me
Unconditionally, you have shown that your love prioritizes me
And, you remind me that God diligently chose you to care for me as such

To experience the protection that your prayers provide
I sense a calmness that is truly beyond my understanding
And, strangely expanding as I travel through life
It is by divine design that your prayers have served as a beam of light

Oh, to know that you are always thinking of me
How blessed is thee who realizes the value of a devoted prayer warrior
A committed and dedicated courier, as God has so ordained you to be
Delightedly, I will forever recall how your prayers have excited my spirit

With Gratitude,
Your Eldest Grandchild

Foreword

Prayer is one of the most important things a Christian can do. It is a time of communicating with God and it should be taken very seriously. While there is deep theological meaning in prayer, it doesn't have to be something that is complicated and difficult. Prayer is something anyone can do anywhere any time.

As you read *"Fill the Gap with Prayer"* by author Drucilla White, you will quickly discover that it is an alphabet of prayers to help ease your burdens. In this book you will find that there are prayers for all generations both young and old. You will learn that prayer is an opportunity to spend time with God.

To really understand the heart of God, you need to pray. In John 15:15, Jesus says He no longer calls us his servants, but calls us His friends. Talking with God helps us to develop a deeper relationship with Him. The deeper the relationship becomes, the more time you will want to spend with Him.

Have you made the mistake of forgetting just how powerful prayer is? When we pray, we are deploying weapons against spiritual battles that linger in dark places. No matter who you are, you have more than likely experienced dark seasons. Dark seasons are the times where the light of day seems so far away. It's the gap we feel when we are disconnected from God. It's idle time spent looking to obtain things that we think will satisfy us.

The author demonstrates throughout this book just how to fill the gap in our lives with the only thing that will help us – prayer. The power of prayer is so great it has the power to defeat the enemy and his power over us. The enemy wants to destroy us, but God wants to bring us closer to Him so he can't. Prayer is our tool to win this battle. Prayer gives us the strength and the faith to finish the race victoriously.

This 30-day prayer book will change our prayer life. The more time we spend with God, the more we are like Him. Our habits and lifestyles will change because prayer changes us from the inside out. In this book you will find protection and experience breakthroughs.

One of the most important aspects of prayer in your life is the breakthroughs that come as a result of it. Sometimes we are faced with devasting circumstances and feel we have nowhere to turn. It is at the point where we can now turn the pages of this book for guidance.

This book was written by one who comes from a family of prayer warriors. There are levels of prayer and the writer operates on the highest level. She is a person of faith with a strong prayer life that has not only changed her life but the lives of many others. You will see testimonies throughout your reading of people who lives have changed because she helped guide them to prayer.

Allow this book to change your life as well by trusting God through the prayers of a Warrior of Prayer.

Pastor Doran Morson, Sr.
Senior Pastor | Higher Praise Worship Center (MI)

Introduction

I absolutely adored my mother and grew up watching her pray about everything. As the youngest of eight children, I saw my parents experience many things and often wondered how did they make it? I watched my mother be a wife, mother and pastor for many years. Prayer began in the early part of my life as a young girl and I too found myself praying about everything, mostly things that revolved <u>around me.</u> As I grew older and got married, I continued my journey with prayer. It was not until after the loss of my father that I started to have a passion for prayer. It was one of the hardest things I would go through in my life. I was only 25 years old when he died and left a large gap in my life and my family's life.

    One of the definitions of a gap according to Merriam - Webster Dictionary is "an incomplete or deficient area". Death of a loved one or someone special can cause a large gap in your life. It's very easy for those gaps to be filled with depression, anger, sadness, guilt and regret. Those are all natural emotions to have given the situation, but if sustained can lead down a dark emotional path. It was through the power of prayer that I was able to survive and grow to understand things in a different way. It was out of this experience that I developed not only a need to pray but a passion to pray.

One of my older sisters that I was close in age with was already a strong prayer warrior and we talked all the time about prayer. I developed a greater passion for prayer during that time and began shifting my focus to praying mostly about things that revolved <u>around others</u>. It was around that time that I accepted the call into ministry. By the age of 31 prayer had become a part of my lifestyle. I incorporated prayer into everything including my marriage and raising my family. Not only through more hurtful loss and pain (loss of first grandchild) did I come to depend on prayer even more for myself, but now more than ever for others. People began to lean on me to help them become more connected to God and fill those gaps in their life and it is through prayer that this can happen.

I was later appointed as the Local Director of Prayer at my church while being the Associate Pastor to my husband. I led a group of prayer warriors every Saturday at noon in prayer time, prayer walks and on evangelistic missions throughout the neighborhood and City of Detroit. This was so successful that I would later be appointed the National Director of Prayer to unite prayer warriors in each local church of the organization.

After prayerfully leaving my birth church in 2002, we no longer had a church body to be a part of or go to. However, I always knew that the church was not in a building but rather a body of believers. It was during this time of spiritual awakening and re-grouping that me and my husband formed and ran prayer cells in our home and in other's homes. It was through these cell groups that believers were strengthened and unbelievers were led to Christ. St. John 15:5 says "I am the vine, ye are the branches: He that abideth in me, and I in him, the same bringeth forth much fruit: for without me ye can do nothing." It is through prayer that we recognize that God wants to use us to help one another.

As Paul wrote in 2 Timothy 3:1 "This know also, that in the last days perilous times shall come." We can say amen to that, those times are here.

We need to be empowered to prosper in the things of God and one way is through having a prayer life. Prayer is the ultimate source of power, because it is the power of the almighty God. God's highest call to each of us is to become a Prayer Warrior. God's promises are to those who overcome and overcomers are men and women of prayer. We must recognize the need for a daily prayer life and prayer time. There will be no harvest until there is prayer for the harvest, St. Matthew 9:38 "Pray ye therefore the Lord of the harvest, that he will send forth labourers into his harvest."

Social Media and the advent of new technologies seek to compete for our time and attention. In our society distractions are plentiful as we experience a 24 hour news cycle, negative reinforcements, and internet influences. Our time is even more precious than ever, so I encourage you to take back control of your time and fill the gap with prayer.

It is within this last year that I created a social media account and was drawn into this phenomenon and quickly discovered its addictive tendencies. Although there are some positive things on social media and inspirational content, THERE IS NO

SUBSTITUTE FOR SPENDING TIME WITH GOD. SO FILL THE GAP WITH PRAYER.

This past year it was made abundantly clear that our lives are filled with so many things that don't necessarily bring us peace and/or spiritual clarity. In the absence of not being able to fill our time and lives with dining out, corporate worship, recreational options and daily living, we were forced to stay at home. If those gaps aren't prioritized with prayer, then they can be filled with loneliness, fear, depression and isolation. During this COVID-19 pandemic we must not be mentally sleep or be unaware, but pray. We must pray through this unprecedented time. There is no time to be spiritually asleep. Wake up and pray!

As I said earlier there are many gaps that need to be filled because of deficiencies. We should take inventory of these gaps in our communities, gaps in our society, gaps in our families and gaps in our lives. It is through sincere prayer that these gaps can be revealed. There are gaps in our love for one another, our patience, and our faith.

Prayer gives us the insight that we need to make it through each day and each decision. Through prayer we reacquaint ourselves with the Holy Spirit, lose sight of our limitations, and experience God's awesome power. Start each day saying "Holy Spirit, here am I please lead and guide me today and let my actions be acceptable unto God."

We pray all the time for change. We want change, but we don't want to change. We must change our priorities, adjust our busy schedules and set aside time alone for prayer. Prayer must become our highest priority.

Today, I live in Delaware where I lead and attend prayer calls with family and other believers each week. Writing this book is another way that God has led me to fulfill his call to raise up prayer warriors all over the United States and the world. I feel it's time to answer that call of God and it begins with YOU.

Prayer should feel natural and not be complicated. Don't worry about not knowing what to say or quoting the right scriptures, just open your heart and let him in. God is ready to commune with you through prayer. I pray that you refer to this book daily or often as possible and then recommend it to someone else. I pray that this book will be a blessing to you and all those you know!

Prayerfully in Service,
Overseer Drucilla White

1

The Author's Prayer

One generation shall praise thy works to another, and shall declare thy mighty acts. **Psalms 145:4 KJV**

Dear Lord God, we lift this younger generation up to you in prayer and faith, knowing that the decisions young people make can affect them for the rest of their lives. Our young people today are tomorrow's leaders. So, we ask that you Lord direct their plans and keep them from evil.

There is a place in God where they can be directed and that place is in prayer. So God, we ask for their hearts to be turned to you and they acknowledge your presence. Lord God, please send laborers to them so they can be mentored in the practice of prayer. God we ask for the prayer anointing to be released on every High School, Middle school, Elementary School, College campuses and even our Medical Schools.

I pray that this book will be an inspiration and guide to help readers make prayer a priority. Lord, teach this younger generation to pray and allow them to be encouraged to put God first in their lives. God please send a Spiritual Awakening among our young people and let them find that place in God where Prayer will calm their minds, guard their spirit, and help them make the right decisions. Keep them from evil, give them wisdom, and help them know who they are in Christ Jesus and embrace their true spiritual identity. This we ask and receive in the name of Jesus the Christ, Amen.

2

Prayer of Repentance

Or despisest thou the riches of his goodness and forbearance and longsuffering; not knowing that the goodness of God leadeth thee to repentance? **Romans 2:4 KJV**

Eternal God, creator of heaven and Earth and all that dwell therein, I stand before you in awe of your majesty and glory. Every part of me worships your presence. I stand before you a broken vessel of clay and ask that you, as the potter, make me over again. I ask your forgiveness for anything that I have done against you or any of your little ones, knowingly or unknowingly. Father God, I repent for the things that I have not done that you commanded me to do.

I repent for not spreading your good tidings by witnessing to the lost as you commanded in St. Matthews 28:19-20 and Acts 1:8. I repent for not showing your love and patience, and for not eating healthy and guarding my temple. I repent for not praying always as you stated in St. Luke 18:1, and for not leading a prayerful life. I repent for disobedience. I repent for the lack of trust, faith and forgiveness in my heart. I repent for how I have handled my tithes and offerings. I repent for broken covenants in marriages, and for broken covenants in being single and raising children. I repent for generational curses that I didn't cease but let live on in me. I repent for unconfessed sins as you provided for me in 2 John 1:9. I repent for not being an example as you said in 1 Timothy 4:12. I repent for not being the mother or father you commanded in your word.

I repent for not studying your word daily to be approved of God. I repent for neglect of worship and praise. I repent for abusing your eternal purpose for the church of which your purpose is to go out and win souls for Jesus Christ. I repent for being a man pleaser and not a lover of God. I repent for not desiring spiritual gifts and grieving the Holy Spirit.

Lastly, I repent for the lack and rejection of knowledge. your word said my people are destroyed for the lack of knowledge, and if I reject knowledge that you would reject me and forget my children.

Cleanse me, wash me, make me clean again. Give me a determined heart to turn all of these things around in my life. I repent, therefore I am revived.

Thank God, and Amen.

3

Prayer of Transformation

Search me, O God, and know my heart: try me, and know my thoughts: And see if there be any wicked way in me, and lead me in the way everlasting. **Psalms 139:23-24 KJV**

Heavenly Father, who is the same yesterday, today and forevermore, incline Thine ear to my prayer of transformation. I pray as King David, create in me a clean heart and renew a right spirit within me. Forgive me of all my transgressions and restore your joy in me. Father God, I ask that you transform me daily by the renewing of my mind that I may rehearse Thy statues and keep Thy law.

Turn the lighthouse in Thy word and shine it on my heart and transform anything that is not like you. Transform me from a peace-breaker to a peacemaker. From a common convert to a dedicated disciple. From an ambassador of discord to an ambassador of love. From a negative thinker to a positive thinker. From a promise breaker to a promise keeper. From an occasional prayer communicator to a prayer warrior. From faithfulness to faithful. From carnal minded to spiritually minded. And, from riotous living to righteous living.

Father God, enter my spirit into a total transformation, according to Thy word, that I may be pleasing in Thy sight. Lastly, make me a product of Thy word as stated in Romans 12:1-2: "I beseech you therefore brethren, by the mercies of God, that you present your bodies a living sacrifice, holy, acceptable unto God, which is your reasonable service. And be not conformed to this world, but be ye transformed by the renewing of your mind, that you may prove what is that good, and acceptable and perfect will of God."

Lord, I thank you for the transformation taking place in my life. This transformation causes me to be different from the world. I have a new way of thinking, a new way of acting, new outlook on life, new strength and new power. I no longer go through the same troubles and despair. When problems come, I face them with the word and the Spirit of God. So, I overcome rather than being overtaken. Again, I thank you for the transformation.

Amen.

4

Prayer for Knowledge and Wisdom

For the Lord giveth wisdom: out of his mouth cometh knowledge and understanding. **Proverbs 2:6 KJV**

Lord Jesus, we ask that you help us to grow in wisdom, knowledge and understanding of you. In the fear of the Lord, we live in awe, filled with reverence of you which motivates us to love and obey.

As we begin to walk in wisdom, draw us and our families near to you. Help us to teach our children to pray. Teach us to be comfortable with talking to you in prayer throughout the day, in all we see, feel, need and celebrate. Also, in all circumstances and decision-making, we want to give praises and thanks for knowing your wisdom will guide us through life when we walk with you.

In Jesus name, Amen.

5

Praise and Thanks

O give thanks unto the Lord ; for he is good: for his mercy endureth for ever. **Psalms 136:1 KJV**

Stop and give thanks for all the days that God has brought us through: death, sickness, viruses troubles, hard times and fear. All of our trials and troubled days come and go, but God's love for us endures forever. His love deserves our enduring thanks and praise. Let us respond with thanks and praise.

Lord Jesus, we profess that you are God; creator and King of the universe and it has been said that our prayers move the hands which move the universe. So God, move our hearts now to exalt you, knowing that your thoughts and ways are higher than ours. Lord God, help us to keep you lifted in our lives, giving thanks from our lips. In our days of trials or triumph, you are worthy of our praise and thanks.

You are not changed by our circumstances and our praise and thanks should not be dependent on them. So when our hearts are heavy as we lift our praises to you, may we always remember your forever love and goodness all of our days. We praise and thank you, God.

Amen.

Testimonies of the Power of Prayer

The Prayer Warrior – Drucilla

I am honored to write about the woman Drucilla whose name means "fruitful" in the Greek language. Early in her walk with God she recognized her strongest gift in the body of Christ was one given to prayer. Indicative of the meaning of her name – much "fruit" has been realized time and time again through her commitment and dedication to prayer. Working in tandem with others she has proven her ability to lead and disciple others by example while being guided by the Holy Spirit. Throughout her ministry she has consistently maintained integrity, compassion, and empathy in forming prayer telephone lines and praying teams both locally and nationally.

I am an eyewitness of how her commitment and dedication to prayer has not only shaped and molded her life over the years but also the lives of countless others. Her approach in prayer displays integrity, love, kindness, **objectivity and empathy** in situations where people want solutions to their problems and comfort in their time of need. They want to experience the power of God in action. One can rest assured that Drucilla can be counted on to be reliable to pray without ceasing until a change comes. **She is indeed, a "Prayer Warrior"!**

Lula White-Odom
Sister In Love

6

Teach us to Pray

And it came to pass, that, as he was praying in a certain place, when he ceased, one of his disciples said unto him, Lord, teach us to pray, as John also taught his disciples. **Luke 11:1 KJV**

Teach us Lord Jesus to pray your heart; for your church and the world around us. Empower us by your spirit, to intercede for others and Your work around the world. May we be one you can call on even in the watches of the night, to build up the wall and stand in the gap on behalf of others. And, may we also respond when you call. Help us, Lord Jesus, to be a watchman for your kingdom.

May we never leave your presence, but learn to worship, fast and continually pray. Teach us what it means to be persistent in prayer until we receive the answers.

Help us to always pray and never give up. Help us to rest before dawn and cry out to you. Help us to always put hope in the promises of Your word.

And, may your word be in our hearts and your promises in our meditations. O' Lord, make us into prayer warriors for your kingdom's sake.

Amen.

7
―――

We Are Overcomers

These things I have spoken unto you, that in me ye might have peace. In the world ye shall have tribulation: but be of good cheer; I have overcome the world. ***John 16:33 KJV***

Father God, your word says that we are overcomers because of the blood of the lamb, the Lord Jesus Christ, and the word of our testimony that is in Jesus.

Thank you, Father God, that because we belong to you in Christ Jesus. You surround us with your presence and you are a wall of fire around us. You, O' Lord, are our refuge and our strength in every situation. Even when we struggle, you are with us and we will not be afraid, for our trust is in Jesus name.

We are always confident that you are with us and will never leave or forsake us. We thank you for your spirit, Lord Jesus, which remains at work in us. Making us to be strong and courageous, as to not be afraid or discouraged. And, always mindful that you are with us, wherever we go. May we also be full of faith and your word, for we belong to you, Jesus Christ.

Amen.

8

Getting in God's Presence Through Prayer

Thou wilt shew me the path of life: in thy presence is fulness of joy; at thy right hand there are pleasures for evermore.
Psalms 16:11 KJV

Lord God Almighty, we praise you because nothing is impossible with you. Train us and lead us into extraordinary prayers. Help us throw off any sins and surrender ourselves completely to you. May we see the needs of our cities and nations the way you see them. Please, unite believers in our churches and communities into extraordinary prayer. Help us to walk in love with each other, agree in our hearts, fast with faith and unite in fervent and persistent prayer.

Lord God, bring revival and spiritual awakening to our land. Lord God, we bring our families before you today; their needs, struggles, goals, concerns, both present and future. Lord, help us to express our gratitude to you by never failing to pray for them to seek your will for their lives. Lord God, give us discernment as to our physical and spiritual needs, in each season. We lift our families up to you in faith, love and in the power of the Holy Spirit. May many generations be blessed because of our prayers. In Jesus name, we pray.

Amen.

9

Make Room for Prayer

But seek ye first the kingdom of God, and his righteousness; and all these things shall be added unto you. **Matthew 6:33 KJV**

God I will make room for you in prayer. Father God we bind the cares of the world and the pride of life. We break every covenant that has been set against the call of God to pray. His word says "Men ought always to pray and not to faint. So we bind all distractions against our private time with God and our prayer assignment. We bind all hindering spirits and we are quickened by the spirit of God to fast, watch, pray, worship and study the word of God in the name of Jesus. We carry the anointing of intercession in our bellies. We will stand in the gap and be on the prayer wall. The word of God says" The Prayer of the righteous avail much."

Thank you God for helping us pray prayers that bring results and avail much.

Amen.

10

Worship Prayer

O come, let us worship and bow down: let us kneel before the Lord our maker. ***Psalms 95:6 KJV***

Heavenly Father, we come to you in the name of Jesus Christ. Lord God, creator of heaven and Earth; as your sons and daughters, we come to worship you as you desire us to, in spirit and in truth. According to the word of God, we know that Jesus Christ is indeed the savior of the world. To our spirit, your spirit witnesses the truth that Jesus is Christ and we believe in Him. Lord God, according to your word, you seek those who worship you and do your will.

Create in us a clean heart, a broken and contrite heart, a right heart and repentance in all our ways. Let nothing be done in strife or vain, but in lowliness of mind, knowing that with you, all things are possible. And with man, the flesh, they shall fall short of your glory.

Lord, we do not come to worship you just to be doing something, but we come to you via the intimate love relationship we have with you through the blood and the cross. Lord God, we choose to abide in the spirit of truth, that we are in a continual state of fellowship and worship with you.
Lord God, our souls hunger and thirst for you, the living God. Lord, we desire you and for your glory to be poured out upon us. Let also your anointing be upon us. Let this be our hearts' cry. Let the fire burn, ever increasing in each one of us. Uphold us with Thy free spirit, and let God be magnified. Lord, if there be any wicked ways within us, let it be exposed and taken out of the way.

We yield ourselves to the Holy Spirit; to worship, honor and praise you. Lord, you will be glorified because you are worthy. Hallelujah.

Amen.

Testimonies of the Power of Prayer

Overseer Drucilla White is a dynamic, power-packed prayer warrior with a call to fortify the Kingdom of God and loosen the bonds of wickedness through her unique ministry. While serving as her Armor Bearer, I found her to be zealous, loyal and willing to give her time and energy to the cause she so strongly believed - which is "PRAYER". Her insights and anointing to teach about going boldly before the throne is sure to take your prayer life to the next level.

Bishop Dr. Aurora L. Jones
Senior Pastor | Church of the Living God (FL)

Overseer White a woman of God who we have had the honor and privilege of witnessing for a number of years as an Intercessor and Prayer Warrior. Psalms 55:17 comes to mind where she cries out to the Lord for others who need prayer, God hears and answers her prayers. As a Prayer Warrior we think of Ezekiel 23:30 where God looked around for one to stand in the gap to war for His people, there is Overseer White. This book is a book of her life and calling.

Pastor Donald and Lady Michalle Warren
Mt. Zion Baptist Church (OH)

11

Let Prayer Arise

But without faith it is impossible to please Him, for he who comes to God must believe that He is, and that He is a rewarder of those who diligently seek Him. **Hebrews 11:6 KJV**

"Now unto him that is able to do exceeding abundantly above all that we ask or think, according to the power that worketh in us." (Ephesians 3:20)

Father God, we thank you for we are the children of the most high God and joint heirs with Christ. We are more than conquerors through Him who loves us. Fear has no place in our lives because God has not given us the spirit of fear, but love, power and a sound mind. We are confident that no weapon formed against us will prosper, because God is for us and so who can be against us? God has blessed us; we are blessed coming out and blessed going in. All that we set our hands to do will prosper and the people of Earth shall see that we are called by the name of the Lord.

We are persuaded that neither death, life, angels, principalities, power, things present, things to come, nor any creature shall be able to separate us from the love of God. We are people of love, as love is shed abroad in our hearts by the Holy Spirit. We thank you, Father, that when we pray, the place in which we assemble will be shaken and we shall all be filled with the Holy Spirit. Your people shall continue to speak the word of God with boldness and courage. Thank You, Father God, that we will let prayer arise and our enemies will be scattered.

Amen.

12

Prayer to Lift Our Younger Generation

One generation commends your works to another; they tell of your mighty acts. ***Psalm 145:4 KJV***

Father God in the name of Jesus Christ we lift up the younger generation in prayer. We declare that they will have a thirst and hunger for the things of God. We release the prayer anointing in the elementary schools, middle schools, high schools, and colleges. God anoint our young people to represent you in the market places, Hollywood political arena and sports arena. We bind the curse of the fatherless generation. We bind every foul spirit of abortion in Jesus name. We bind every pervert spirit that will come against our younger generation. Pornography, incest, rape, sexual crimes, spirit of violation, devil you will not steal the purity of this younger generation. We declare that every wicked imagination that tried to exalt itself against the knowledge of God is stricken and destroyed in Jesus name. We declare that this younger generation will not be ashamed of the gospel of Jesus Christ they will shine as a light on the top of a hill and draw others into God's kingdom. We bind the spirit of rebellion, suicide, alcohol drug uses every door to the demonic is closed through music, movies, videos games and internet we pray to God that this younger generation will be focused and steadfast in the Lord Jesus Christ. Amen.

13

Healing Prayer

Heal me, O Lord , and I shall be healed; save me, and I shall be saved: for thou art my praise. **Jeremiah 17:14 KJV**

Heavenly Father, in accordance with the excellence of your word, we pray that you will heal our bodies of all affliction and restore our health. We need your help and pray your word that our needs be met. It is in the powerful name of Jesus that we pray these prayers to you. Amen.

"For I will restore health unto thee, and I will heal thee of thy wounds…" (Jeremiah 30:17 KJV)

"If thou wilt diligently hearken to the voice of the Lord thy God, and wilt do that which is right in his sight, and wilt give ear to his commandments, and keep all his statutes, I will put none of these diseases upon thee…" (Exodus 15:26 KJV)

"But he was wounded for our transgressions, he was bruised for our iniquities; the chastisement for our peace was upon him, and with his stripes we are healed." (Isaiah 53:5 KJV)

"Who forgiveth all thine iniquities, who healeth all thy diseases. Who reedemeth thy life from destruction, who crowneth thee with loving-kindness and tender mercies…" (Psalm 103:3-4 KJV)

"Who his own self bare our sins in his own body on the tree, that we, being dead to sins, should live unto righteousness; by whose stripes ye were healed." (1 Peter 2:24 KJV)

"Beloved, I wish above all things that thou mayest prosper and be in health, even as thy soul prospereth." (3 John 1:2 KJV)

Amen.

14

Prayer Warrior's Confession

But we will give ourselves continually to prayer, and to the ministry of the word. ***Acts 6:4 KJV***

Our Father, we come before you in the name of Jesus Christ, our Lord. We thank you and praise you for all of your mighty works. We recognize that you are God and besides you, there is none other. You made the heavens and the Earth and everything that is therein. In you we live, we move and have our being.

Lord, we present ourselves unto you holy and acceptable, so that you may use us for your honor and glory. Father God, forgive and cleanse us of all sin and unrighteousness, so that we may be worthy to partake of all Thy goodness and glory. Father God, we ask that you be partakers with us, giving love, wisdom, knowledge, understanding, faith, power and authority granted unto us as Thy servants. We ask for courage and boldness to speak Thy words through our prayers and the stretching forth of our hands, that signs and wonders be done in the name of Jesus Christ.

Father, we ask that you receive these prayer warriors, as we bind together in unity of our love for you almighty God, as well as love and compassion for mankind. That we will be a channel for you to use in order to reach mankind, who you love so much.

We stand in agreement according to your word, that where two or three agree on Earth touching anything that they shall ask, and it shall be done for them by my Father who is in heaven. And when we pray, we believe and we receive because your word has gone out and it will not return void; but, accomplish the things whereunto it was sent. Your word said that if we ask anything according to your will, you will hear us and if we know that you hear us whatsoever we ask, we know that we have the petition that we desire of you.

So we know that you hear us almighty God because your word said the eyes of the Lord is over the righteous and His ears are open to their prayers.

Lord, we thank you and ask that you grant unto us the faith, word of knowledge, hope, patience and courage to stand in the face of the evidence of answered prayers.

Amen.

15

Prayer According to Ephesians 1:17-22

That the God of our Lord Jesus Christ, the Father of glory, may give unto you the spirit of wisdom and revelation in the knowledge of him: ***Ephesians 1:17 KJV***

Father, we pray that you will grant us today, this day, the spirits of wisdom and revelation in the knowledge of the Lord Jesus Christ. Oh, that the eyes of our understanding may be enlightened. That the eyes of our hearts may be flooded with light. That we may know the hope of your calling, Father. That we may know what is the richest of the glory of your inheritance in the saints, and that we may know the exceeding greatness of your power towards us as believers. We want you to know it today. We want to have the spirits of wisdom and revelation today in the knowledge of Christ. We want to have the eyes of our understanding and hearts flooded with light today. Today, we want to know the hope of His calling. Today, we want to know what is the richest of the glory of His inheritance in us, His saints. Today, we want to know the exceeding greatness of His power towards us as believers. We want that resurrection power, today.

Amen.

Testimonies of the Power of Prayer

Drucilla White has been a Prayer Warrior for decades. When this woman of prayer connects in the spirit with God you will experience powerful life changing results.

1st **Lady Sylvia Morson**
Higher Praise Worship Center (MI)

Mama White as we fondly call her is a woman of exceeding grace, wisdom and virtue. Both in our personal lives, and so many other areas, Mama White has always stepped up to lead us in various seasons of warfare prayers and we have consistently witnessed great victories under her prayer ministry.

Tobi and Nike Adegoke
Producer & Minister of Music

16
───

Prayer Covering

He shall cover thee with his feathers, and under his wings shalt thou trust: his truth shall be thy shield and buckler.
Psalms 91:4 KJV

Dear Heavenly Father, we pray this prayer covering in the power of the Holy Spirit and in the name of Jesus Christ. We bind, rebuke, remove and bring to no effect, all division, discord, strife, anger, wrath, murder, criticism, pride, envy, jealousy, gossip, slander, evil speaking, complaining, lying, false teaching, false gifts, poverty, fear of lack, fear of spirits, murmuring spirits, complaining spirits, hindering spirits, deceiving spirits, occult spirits, witchcraft spirits and spirts of the anti-Christ. We bind in the name of Jesus, all curses that have been spoken against us. We bless those who curse us and pray blessings on those who despitefully use us. We bind the power of negative words from others and we bind and render useless, all prayers not inspired by the Holy Spirit.

We are the children of God, we resist the devil, and he does flee from us. No weapon formed against thee shall prosper, and every tongue that shall rise against thee in judgement, thou shalt condemn. This is the heritage of the servants of the Lord, and their righteousness is of us, saith the Lord. We put on the whole armor of God and we take authority in Jesus name and let it be prosperous for us. Let us walk in your love, Lord.

Holy Spirit, lead and guide us always. Let us discern between the righteous and the wicked. We pray for your anointing to be on every word that you have designed and created and spoken for such a time as this. We will keep your word in the midst of our hearts, for they are life unto those that find them and health to all their flesh. We invite your spirit, patience and love into every circumstance that you may be great in the midst of thee.

We ask this prayer in the name of Jesus. Thank God, and Amen.

17

Prayer for the Nation

The Lord is nigh unto all them that call upon him, to all that call upon him in truth. **Psalms 145:18 KJV**

Lord Jesus, thank you for hearing our prayers. We thank you for the door your blood has formed, leading us to the throne room of heaven. To cry out and know that our heavenly Father inclines His ear to His children as we repent and seek your face with praise and thanksgiving.

Thank you for your patience and your long suffering with us so that we do not perish in our pride and sin. We are reminded again to humble ourselves and return to You, your word, your will, and your ways. Lord, this is our prayer for America, our families, and each one of us. That we would know you, reflect upon your word and worship you, in spirit and in truth. Pour out your presence, your peace and the knowledge of the glory of the Lord, on our nation. In the name of Jesus, we pray.

Amen.

18

Rededication Prayer

Humble yourselves therefore under the mighty hand of God, that he may exalt you in due time: Casting all your care upon him; for he careth for you. **1 Peter 5:6-7 KJV**

As we rededicate our lives to the Lord Jesus Christ, we confess that Jesus is Lord over our spirits, souls and bodies.

As we reclaim Jesus as the head of our lives, we confess Jesus has been made unto us: wisdom, righteousness, sanctification and redemption. We can do all things through Christ, who strengthens us. "As [we] reclaim Jesus as Lord, [we] do not fret or have anxiety about anything; [we] do not have a care" (Phil. 4:6).

The Lord is our shepherd, we do not want. Our God supplies all our needs according to his riches in glory in Christ Jesus. As we rededicate our lives to the Lord, the love of god has been shed abroad in our hearts, by the Holy Spirit and his love abides in us richly. "[We] keep ourselves in the kingdom of light in love in the word and the wicked one toucheth [us] not" (Romans 5:5, I John 4:16, 5:18).

We are delivered from this present evil world. We are seated with Christ in heavenly places. We reside in the kingdom of God's dear son. The law of the spirit of life in Christ Jesus has made us free from the laws of sin and death.

As we rededicate our lives to the Lord, we are not conformed to this world but are transformed by the renewing of our minds. That we may prove what is the good, acceptable and perfect will of God. As we rededicate our lives, we are useful members in the body of Christ. We are his workmanship, recreated in Christ Jesus. "[Our] Father God is all the while effectual at work in both to will and to do his good pleasure" (I John 5:4-5, Eph. 2:10, Phil. 2:13).

"[We] let the word dwell in us richly. He who began a good work in [us] will continue until the day of Christ" (Col. 3:16, Phil. 1:1-6).

Praise God that we are rededicated to the Lord Jesus Christ.

Amen.

19

Prayer for Pastors

I exhort therefore, that, first of all, supplications, prayers, intercessions, and giving of thanks, be made for all men; For kings, and for all that are in authority; that we may lead a quiet and peaceable life in all godliness and honesty.
1 Timothy 2:1-2 KJV

Father God, we thank you that our pastors are filled with the spirits of wisdom and revelation, in the knowledge of you. Continue to help these pastors and leaders in fulfilling Your perfect plan for their lives. We pray that the spirits of wisdom and knowledge will guide them in every meeting, activity and conversation that they engage in. We thank you for their prayerful life. We ask you to protect them from all hurt, harm and danger. We ask that you keep them from sickness, poverty, fear and oppression, that these things may have no power over them.

Give them divine health and rest, that they may be refreshed. We ask that no weapon formed against them shall prosper and that every lying tongue that comes against them, shall be silenced. We ask that you give them favor in every business deal and in every opportunity that comes their way.

We cancel every attack of the wicked one to bring deception, distractions, hindrance and temptation into their lives. Devil, you are bound and have no authority over these pastors and leaders, or their families nor their possessions.

We ask that you cover these pastors and leaders, with the blood of Jesus and with our prayers, we ask that you release angels of God to protect them every day of their lives.

Lord God, we ask that these pastors and leaders continue to set new and good standings of excellence for the body of Christ. That they be led by the leading of the Holy Spirit and that they remain faithful and obedient to the Holy Spirit. In Jesus name, Amen.

20

Prayer According to Philippians 4:6-8

Be careful for nothing; but in every thing by prayer and supplication with thanksgiving let your requests be made known unto God. ***Philippians 4:6 KJV***

God is healing us and inspiring us; guiding and strengthening us. So we are careful for nothing, but in everything by prayer and supplication. With thanksgiving, we will let our request be made known unto God, and His peace which passeth all of our understanding will keep our hearts and minds close to Christ Jesus. So whatsoever things are true, hopeful, just, pure, lovely and good, we will think on these things. In Jesus name, Amen.

Testimonies of the Power of Prayer

Drucilla White is truly a woman of God who has been standing in the gap as a prayer warrior for many years. Back in the late seventies and early eighties, the Lord led her to start a prayer team at the church where we both attended; which she did. I was blessed to be one of the ones she chose to be on the team. The team met together every week at the church for prayer. I've had the opportunity for over forty years to witness this woman of God pray, weep, wail, and mourn in intercession for others. I believe she has a lot to say about prayer and I believe this book will be a blessing to everyone who reads it.

May God continue to bless this woman of God as she continues to intercede for others.

Ida M. Williams
Author of religious material

21

Praise Prayer

Rejoice in the Lord, O ye righteous: for praise is comely for the upright. ***Psalms 33:1 KJV***

Father God, this is the day that the Lord has made. We will rejoice and be glad in it. We rejoice in you always; again, we say rejoice!

The joy of the Lord is our strength. We have victory in the name of Jesus. Satan is under our feet. Greater is he who is in us than he who is in the world. We are believers not doubters. We can do all things through Christ who strengthens us.

We do not fret or have anxiety about anything. We do not have a care. We cast our cares upon the Lord Jesus, for He cares for us.

So let us magnify the Lord and let us exalt his name together. Let us praise His holy name. Let us give Him thanks, for He is worthy of all our praise. Let the words of our mouths and the meditations of our hearts be acceptable in your sight.

Bless the Lord, oh our souls, and all that is within us. Bless your holy name. We worship and adore you. You are the everlasting God, the great God, the living God, the merciful God, the faithful God, the mighty God. We will bless the Lord at all times. His praises shall continually be in our mouths. Let God arise, and let his enemies be scattered.

Praise ye the Lord. O' give thanks unto the Lord for He is good, and his mercy endureth forever.

Make a joyful noise unto the Lord all ye lands. Serve the Lord with gladness. Come before His presence with singing, enter into His gates with thanksgiving, and into his courts with praise. Be thankful unto Him and bless His holy name.

Amen.

22

A Prayer of Faith

Bless the Lord, O' my soul, and forget not all his benefits.

Psalm 103:2 KJV

Lord, in obedience to Your word, we recall and receive a new today all the benefits Jesus has provided for us.

He has forgiven all my sins. He is our healer, and we receive our healing and health today. Our lives are redeemed from destruction. We are crowned with His loving-kindness and tender mercies. He satisfies our mouths with good things so that our youth is renewed like the eagle's. He executeth righteousness and judgement for us against oppression. We are free.

He makes known His ways to us. We are His children and we follow him.

We receive His grace and mercy and obtain it in times of need.

Amen.

23

Extraordinary Prayer

And he said, The things which are impossible with men are possible with God. ***Luke 18:27 KJV***

Lord God Almighty, we praise you and nothing is impossible with you. Train us and lead us into extraordinary prayer. Help us throw off any sin, thereby surrendering ourselves completely to you. May we see the needs of our communities and nation the way you see them. Unite believers in our churches and communities in extraordinary prayer. May we walk in love. Agree in heart and spirit. Fast in faith and unite in fervent, persistent prayer. Lord God Almighty, bring revival and spiritual awakening to our lands. Be glorified through us, O' Lord.

Father God, we thank you that you sent Jesus to seek and to save that which was lost. Therefore in the name of Jesus, we claim souls into your kingdom.

Amen.

24

Prayer of Confessions

But what saith it? The word is nigh thee, even in thy mouth, and in thy heart: that is, the word of faith, which we preach;
Romans 10:8 KJV

Father, because of your word we have the spirits of wisdom and revelation in the knowledge of God. So we covenant with you now to always give voice to your word. We will never give back to the words of the enemy. We give no place to the devil. But we give place to the spirit of God. You have given the angels charge over us in all ways and our ways is the way of the word of God.

These things we pray will surely come to pass. For your word is within us. We have been delivered from the power of darkness and translated into the kingdom of the Son of God. The Greater One dwells within us, so we will not fail. For your word is within is.

Your word will cause us to prevail, even though a thousand may fall and the ten thousand at our right hand. It shall not come near us for you've given your angels charge over us to keep us. Heavenly Father, we make a covenant with you to voice your words. The spirit of truth within us will guide us into all truths. He will teach us all things and show us what rightfully belongs to us. We proclaim the promises of God are ours now. Amen.

25

Authority Prayer

These things speak, and exhort, and rebuke with all authority. Let no man despise thee. ***Titus 2:15 KJV***

In the name of Jesus Christ, we address and take authority over the Prince of Power of the air. And over the principalities, evil powers, the rulers of darkness of this world and spiritual wickedness in high places. Those of which have been assigned by Satan to terrorize God-fearing people and the government.

Satan, we bind your works and render them null and void in the name of Jesus. We forbid you to operate in this world. We cast you and your demons our of our land, county, and the country.

For we know this, that God is for us, and if God be for us, who can be against us? We shall not be afraid of the terrors of the night nor the arrow the evil plots. Nor the slanders of the wicked that which flies by day. Nor of the pestilence that stalks in darkness. Nor the destruction and sudden death that lay waste at noon day.

Therefore we establish ourselves as righteous, in conformity with God's will and order. We shall be far from the thoughts of oppression or destruction, for we shall not fear. And from terror, for it shall not come near us.

Holy Spirit, thank you for writing this word upon the tablets of our hearts so that we can speak it out of our mouths. For we will order our conversations aright and you will show us, your people, the salvation of God. Hallelujah, and Amen.

Testimonies of the Power of Prayer

It is my distinct honor as a personal witness of the powerful gift of prayer that mom White possess. Recently she prayed for me regarding healing in my body. The power of God was so strong I didn't need to have surgery. I'm truly grateful for her commitment to the call on her life. I'm a walking witness.

Tina Williams (Psalmist)

Overseer White has dedicated her life to being a Prayer Warrior. When I was sick, she prayed and encouraged me as healing began to manifest in my body. James 5:16 states," The effectual, fervent prayer of a righteous man availeth much". Overseer White shares her knowledge of how through prayer, you can develop an intimate relationship with God and experience His glory.

Crystal Barnett (Prayer Warrior)

Mom White is a strong woman of God, she's a prayer warrior that knows how to bring the Word of God to manifest. When she prays the anointing of God sets the atmosphere to let people know that God do exist as we walk by faith with God's Word coming alive right before your eyes. When she prays the Lord listens and always moves on her behalf because her prayers are love letters to God for Him to perform His Works for His people.

Tamara H. Swain, M.Ed (Prayer Warrior)

Prayer for a New Year 2021

But thou, O Lord, art a shield for me; my glory, and the lifter up of mine head. ***Psalms 3:3 KJV***

He shall cover thee with his feathers, and under his wings shalt thou trust: his truth shall be thy shield and buckler. (Psalms 91:4) We thank God that we have come out of a year of many changes, people dying by the thousands from the Corona virus. A year where the schools closed, churches closed, and businesses closed. We were forced to have funerals in a new way and could not visit our loved ones in the hospitals and nursing homes.

We thank God we made it through....

Now for the New Year, we ask God for his protection, peace, his presence with the each of us in the New Year. The word of God says first offer prayer intercession and giving of thanks be made for all men, kings and for all that are in authority. God we ask you for your protection to be upon our nation, president, our first black women vice president, all heads of state, all lawmakers, Police officials, and military personal. In the midst of a divided nation we need God's peace and healing in our world. Helps us to demonstrate justice and unity for all people with extraordinary love. Amen.

27

Authority in Jesus Christ

Behold I give unto you power to tread on serpents and scorpions, and over all the power of the enemy, and nothing shall by any means hurt you. **Luke 10:19 KJV**

We cast down imagination and every high thing that exalteth itself against the knowledge of God, and bring into captivity every thought to the obedience of Christ. (2 Corinthians 10:5) In the name of Jesus Christ , Our Lord and Savior. We take authority over the prince of power of the air and over the principalities, evil powers. Rulers of darkness of this world and spiritual wickedness in high places who have been assigned by satan to intimidate, frighten and oppress God's people and the government.

Satan we bind your works and render them null and void in the name of Jesus Christ. We forbid you to operate in this world, we cast you and your demons out of our land. We know that God is for us and if God be for us who can be against us. We shall not be afraid of the terror by night nor the arrow, the evil plots and slander of the wicked. Therefore we take authority in Jesus name. God order our steps, Holy Spirit thank you for writing the words of God upon our hearts, so we can speak it out of our mouths, and the Lord God said he will hasten his word to perform it...thank you Jesus....Hallelujah!!!!

28

Prayer Will Change Things

And at midnight Paul and Silas prayed, and sang praises unto God: and the prisoners heard them. And suddenly there was a great earthquake, so that the foundations of the prison were shaken: and immediately all the doors were opened, and every one's bands were loosed. ***Act 16:25-26 KJV***

Father God your word says, "Men ought always to pray and not faint, so if we don't pray we will pay, because prayer can't wait. Prayer is power, no prayer no power, little prayer, little power, much prayer much power. Prayer bring us into unique fellowship with the Godhead, God the father, God the Son, God the Holy Spirit.

Prayer and intercession are powerful weapons in the hands of prayer warriors, intercessors, and believers of God. Prayer stops the plans of satan against our lives and our families life. Prayer establishes God's plan in our life and the lives of our love ones.

We will not put Prayer on hold, because prayer changes things for the better. Praise God!!

29

Who Am I, My True Identity

The Spirit itself beareth witness with our spirit, that we are the children of God: **Romans 8:16 KJV**

Lord Jesus this is a question each one of us should ask ourselves, Who am I, Father God because we are carnally minded, we would answer, with our name and where we live. But Lord Jesus who are we and what is our true identity, only in the person of Jesus Christ would we find the answer.

The bible reveals we are Spirit. Soul and body Lord help us to feed our Spirits with the word of God as much as we feed our body, then we will realize who we are..

The Word of God tell us we are children of God according to Romans 8:16, it tell us we are heir of God and joint heir with Christ Jesus according Romans 8:17

We have been saved by Grace through faith in Jesus Christ. We have been redeemed from the hand of the enemy and we are more than Conquerors. We are the righteousness of God in Christ Jesus.

So light up the World with who you are in Jesus Christ and fill the gap with Prayer. Amen.

30

Pleading the Blood of Jesus

And the blood shall be to you for a token upon the houses where ye are: and when I see the blood, I will pass over you, and the plague shall not be upon you to destroy you, when I smite the land of Egypt. **Exodus 12:13 KJV**

Father God we plead the Blood of Jesus over our entire household, Lord cover our relatives. Friend and their families. We plead the blood of Jesus over all ministries, Lord cover your blood over every Pastor, Minister, Apostle, Prophet, Evangelist and Teacher in this Nation. We plead the Blood of Jesus over the entire body of Christ.

Satan in the name of Jesus we bind you and every principality, power, ruler of darkness and spiritual wickedness in high places. We bind every evil spirit, demon spirit, and every spirit that is not of God. We cancel every assignment of satan in Jesus Name.

No weapon that is formed against us shall prosper every lying tongue is silenced and every enemy that rises up against us is smitten before our face and flees before us seven ways.

As we fill the gaps with prayer, we bind, rebuke and cast out the spirit of fear, doubt, worry, unbelief and give them no place in our lives.

We pull down all strongholds and cast down every vain and wicked imagination exalting itself against the knowledge of God and bring every thought captive to the obedience of Jesus Christ... AMEN

www.ingramcontent.com/pod-product-compliance
Lightning Source LLC
Chambersburg PA
CBHW031214090426
42736CB00009B/917